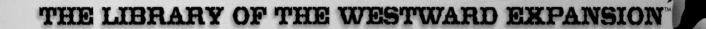

THE LIBRARY OF THE WESTWARD EXPANSION™

THE QUEST FOR
California's Gold

James P. Burger

For Judith, who started me on my own hunt

Published in 2002 by The Rosen Publishing Group, Inc.
29 East 21st Street, New York, NY 10010

Copyright © 2002 by The Rosen Publishing Group, Inc.

First Edition

Book Design: Emily Muschinske
Project Editor: Kathy Campbell

Photo Credits: pp. 5 (map), 14 (cartoon), 18 (mine) © The Granger Collection, New York; p. 5 (mill) © Robert Holmes/CORBIS; p, 5 (gold) © Roger Garwood & Trish Ainslie/CORBIS; p. 6 (dreamer) © The Huntington Library, Art Collections, and Botanical Gardens, San Marino, CA/SuperStock; p. 6 (mining town) © Museum of History & Industry/CORBIS; pp. 9 (children), 21 © Archive Photos; pp. 9 (forty-niners), 14 (panning for gold), 18 (gamblers) © SuperStock; p. 10 (map) Santi Visalli/Archive Photos; p. 10 (Chinese immigrants) © American Stock/Archive Photos; p. 13 © Hulton Getty/Archive Photos; p. 14 (miner with mule) © The Huntington Library; p. 17 © Bettmann/CORBIS.

Burger, James P.
    The quest for California's gold / James P. Burger — 1st ed.
            p. cm. — (The library of the westward expansion)
Includes index.
  ISBN 0–8239–5849–3 (lib. bdg.)
 1. California—Gold discoveries—Juvenile literature. 2. Frontier and pioneer life—California—Juvenile literature. 3. California—History—1846–1850—Juvenile literature. [1. California—Gold discoveries. 2. California—History—1846–1850. 3. Frontier and pioneer life—California.]
I. Title.
  F865 .B94 2002
  979.4'04—dc21   00–011693

Manufactured in the United States of America

Contents

A Valuable Discovery

Until the late 1840s, California was **wilderness**. It belonged to Mexico. Then the United States won it when the Mexican-American War ended on February 2, 1848.

The people living in California before it became a U.S. **territory** were mostly Native Americans. Some were Mexican cowboys. During the early 1800s, a few Americans and Europeans settled there. A German, John Sutter, owned a fort where the city of Sacramento is today. He also owned a vineyard, orchards, and a **tannery**. He wanted a sawmill and hired a carpenter, James Marshall, to build it. On January 24, 1848, Marshall saw little, shiny stones on the bottom of a river near the building **site**. He took a few stones to Sutter. To everyone's surprise, Marshall had found gold nuggets!

Right: *Sutter's Fort, seen here, became a popular place to stop in Sacramento during gold miners' search for gold.*

Top: *This map from 1851 shows how land was divided in the United States and the territories around it, including California, Oregon, and Mexico.*

Lower Right: *The gold nuggets that James Marshall discovered while building Sutter's Mill might have looked similar to these.*

Left: A California miner dreams about prospecting for gold.

Right: This picture of Skagway, Alaska, from 1898 shows what a mining town looked like. Many stores sold supplies to gold miners for digging their claims.

Gold Fever

Word of Sutter's gold appeared in a newspaper called the *Californian* on March 15, 1848. Sam Brannan, owner of another newspaper as well as some stores, saw an **opportunity**. He ran through the streets of San Francisco carrying a bottle of gold dust. "Gold! Gold!" he yelled. "Gold from the American River!" He hoped to attract people to the area so they would shop at his stores. By 1849, it seemed as if the entire world had been struck by gold fever. Today gold is still very valuable because it is **scarce**. Millions of dollars of gold lay buried around Sutter's Mill and Native American villages such as those of the Miwok and Yokut.

Above: *This drawing of Sutter's Mill, where the first gold was discovered, appeared in John Sutter's book about the discovery.*

DID YOU KNOW?

The first gold rushers to arrive headed straight for Sutter's Mill, where they set up camps and began to dig. Within days, much of Sutter's land was destroyed by gold seekers.

The Race to California

Shopkeepers, teachers, doctors, and others left their jobs to become **prospectors**. Even women and children were allowed to prospect for gold. Freed slaves worked beside whites. Asians, Europeans, and South Americans also arrived to try their luck in the Sierra Nevada **foothills** of northern California.

No one expected that so many would respond to the news about gold in California. In 1849, nearly 90,000 people headed there. They became known as the forty-niners. During the next 10 years, another 375,000 people from more than 70 nations arrived in California. Most forty-niners took long ship voyages to the California goldfields. Others already lived in the western United States and could cross the western territories in covered wagon trains. Both ways took a long time and involved many dangers.

Below: *This image shows children cradling for gold in a stream. In this process, one person puts soil from the river into a cradle while another person moves it back and forth in the flow of the water. Gold is caught by a screen or shovel placed below.*

Above: *Forty-niners mine for gold. Many gold seekers came to California from faraway places, such as China and Europe.*

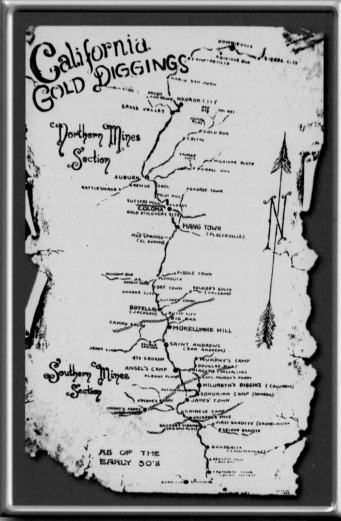

California Gold Diggings

Northern Mines Section

Southern Mines Section

AS OF THE EARLY 50'S

Above: This map from the 1850s shows many of the important mines in California during the gold rush period.

Below: These Chinese immigrants have just arrived in northern California to seek their fortunes in mining for gold. For most forty-niners, California was the first place where they had seen so many people from different countries.

Routes by Ship

People traveling by ship had a choice between two routes. People taking the shortest route from the East Coast of the United States sailed through the Caribbean Sea and docked in eastern Panama in about a month. Then they had to cross a dangerous jungle filled with alligators and mosquitoes to reach the Pacific Ocean. Those who **survived** took another ship to go north the rest of the way to California. Travelers going by the longer sea route sailed around Cape Horn, the tip of South America. For three to six months, they had to suffer rough storms, seasickness, and lack of fresh water, fruit, and vegetables.

DID YOU KNOW?

A steamship named the *California* reached the mines first, on February 28, 1849. Right away, the crew left it to search for gold. San Francisco's bay soon was filled with empty ships.

The Overland Trails

In 1849, about 23,000 people rode to the goldfields in covered wagons. They set out from places such as Saint Joseph, Missouri, and Council Bluffs, Iowa, to cross the prairies of the Midwest. After the three-month crossing, the trail grew bumpy. During the trip across the hot deserts of the American West, water and supplies ran low. People died of thirst. Many oxen, mules, and horses that pulled the covered wagons also died.

After these **hardships** of the desert, the forty-niners had to cross the high Sierra Nevada mountain range to reach California. Crossing this range in the winter was too dangerous. People had tried, but many never made it to the other side. Travelers who arrived at the mountains just before winter had to camp through the season.

Right: *A wagon tries to make the trip over the Sierra Nevada mountains during the California gold rush.*

Top: *This wagon train is making its way through the Sierra Nevada mountains and has reached Swift's Station. Travelers could stay here in a lodge before making their way to other mining towns.*

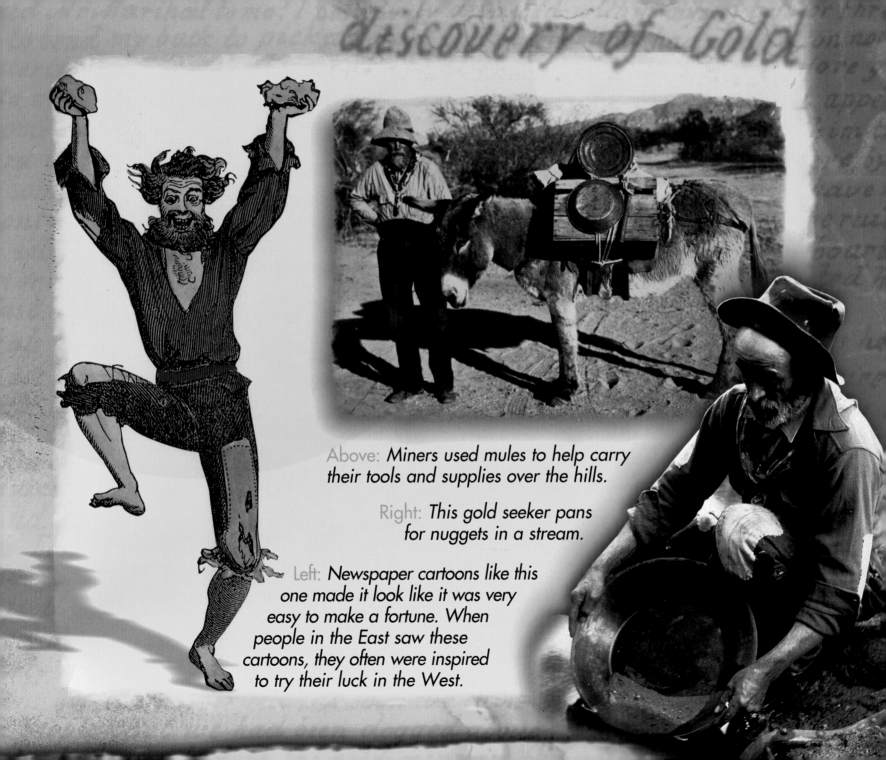

Above: *Miners used mules to help carry their tools and supplies over the hills.*

Right: *This gold seeker pans for nuggets in a stream.*

Left: *Newspaper cartoons like this one made it look like it was very easy to make a fortune. When people in the East saw these cartoons, they often were inspired to try their luck in the West.*

Life in the Goldfields

People heard **exaggerated** tales about the gold waiting to be found in California. Newspapers even told of streams paved with gold! Everyone who arrived, whether black, white, Asian, man, woman, or child, expected to get rich easily. What they found in the mines was another story.

Early in the gold rush, much gold lay throughout the Sierra Nevada foothills. People raced to reach the treasure first. Prospectors often would work long hours, lifting heavy stones but finding very little of the **precious** metal. Some turned to crime, trying to collect easy gold by robbing others. People in the mining camps soon needed lawmen to help keep order.

DID YOU KNOW?

One gold rush story tells of three Frenchmen who dug up a tree stump from a road near Sutter's Fort. When they lifted it out of the ground, they found $5,000 worth of gold nuggets!

Tools of the Trade

When the gold rush began, much gold lay in the American River like loose stones, just as James Marshall had discovered it. Miners panned for the gold. They scooped the river's sand into their tin pans, then washed it again and again. Water spilled out, taking the sand with it. Gold, too heavy to be washed away, stayed behind in the pans. Forty-niners also made long slides, called **sluices**. They built them across a bend in a stream. The river flowed through the sluices while the owners shoveled gravel into them. Just like it did with pans, gold remained in the bottoms of the sluices waiting to be claimed. By 1852, most of the gold that could be found on the surface had been taken. Mining companies dug deep mines to reach what gold was left in the hills, even though this was dangerous work. Soon even that gold from underground was taken.

Right: *This man has a pan, a bag for his nuggets, and a jug for water. He wears a hat with a wide brim to protect him from the heat or rain.*

Above: *Gold miners used axes, hoes, picks, and shovels as tools for digging in the hills and streams of California.*

Above: *This picture from 1877 shows the inside of an underground mine. The wooden beams helped make it safe for the miners to dig for gold below the town. At the top of the picture, part of the boomtown can be seen.*

Cities and Boomtowns

Thousands with gold fever crowded the town of San Francisco. Bankers, doctors, and lawyers alike wore dusty work clothes instead of suits. People wildly bought supplies before staking claims in the hills. San Francisco quickly became a crowded city. Before the gold rush, only 800 people had lived there. During the 1850s, hundreds more sailed into its bay daily. Smaller towns, called boomtowns, were started closer to the mines. They offered the miners supplies, tools, and entertainment. Saloons and gambling halls gave miners a break from their hardships. The towns had wild names such as Chicken Thief Flat and You Bet!

Left: *Boomtowns had saloons, such as this one from 1907, and gambling halls, where the miners could go for entertainment.*

DID YOU KNOW?

A city called Sacramento grew around Sutter's Fort. On September 9, 1850, California became the thirty-first state of the United States. Sacramento was made the state's capital in 1854.

Other Golden Chances

Not many people struck it rich during the California gold rush. There was gold in the hills, but there were too many people **competing** for it. Gold became harder to find as thousands of people dug in the rivers and made the water muddier every day. Most of the people who struck it rich, though, did not dig for gold. Wise businessmen, like Sam Brannan, charged high prices for their valuable goods and skills. Women ran restaurants, in which the miners could enjoy a hot meal that tasted better than the food in their camps. Even some children started their own businesses, selling newspapers in the streets. One man, Levi Strauss, came to California with plans to sell sturdy tents. Strauss met a miner who needed strong, heavy pants. Strauss cut his tent fabric and made a pair. Soon he was selling these denim pants to many of the miners. Today Levi's "blue jeans" are sold all over the world.

Right: In 1899, men in Alaska paid for their supplies in gold dust, using a special scale. Using gold dust and nuggets instead of money was allowed in boomtowns.

When the Excitement Ended

By 1859, after 10 years of digging for gold in California, most people gave up their search. In the spring of 1859, Henry Comstock stumbled on great riches while exploring the Great Basin in Nevada. This time it was silver, and it was named the Comstock Lode. Many of the forty-niners staked new claims in Nevada, and so the California gold rush ended. The gold rush had ruined John Sutter's life. His land had been torn apart by the miners who had overrun California. Both Sutter and Marshall went into the goldfields, too, but they never had any luck. The local Native Americans were left to repair their villages. The unwelcome miners had destroyed the Native Americans' lives and homes. In the end, some miners returned to the homes they had left. Many had become poor, and work was often hard to find. Those who stayed in California became the first citizens of the most **populated** state in the United States today.

Glossary

competing (kum-PEET-ing) Trying hard to win something.

exaggerated (ihg-ZAH-juh-rayt-ed) When a statement has been blown up to make it seem greater, more important, or more interesting than it really is.

foothills (FUT-hilz) Hills at the base of a mountain range.

hardships (HARD-ships) Events or actions that cause suffering.

opportunity (ah-per-TOO-nih-tee) A good chance.

populated (PAH-pyoo-layt-ed) Having people living there.

precious (PREH-shus) Having a high value or price.

prospectors (prah-SPEK-terz) People who explore an area for minerals such as gold.

scarce (SKAIRS) Small in amount and hard to find but wanted very much.

site (SYT) The place where a builder chooses to build.

sluices (SLOO-sez) Man–made passages for water.

survived (sur-VYVD) To have lived longer than; to have stayed alive.

tannery (TA-nuh-ree) A place where animal skins are made into leather that can be used.

territory (TEHR-uh-tohr-ee) Land that is controlled by a person or a group of people.

wilderness (WIL-dur-nis) An area that is wild and has no permanent settlements.

Index

Web Sites

To learn more about the quest for California's gold, check out these Web sites:

www.huntington.org/Education/GoldRush/index.html
www.pbs.org/goldrush/funfacts.html
www.pbs.org/wgbh/amex/kids/goldrush/